PENGUIN BOOKS

Country Women's Association

Cakes

TRADITIONAL, TEMPTING, TRIED-AND-TRUE

PENGUIN BOOKS

Contents

Foreword

The Country Women's Association of Australia has been in existence for more than 80 years and its members have long had a reputation for being wonderful cooks. Indeed, too often it seems that the public and the media think that our main activity is 'making tea and scones', though this is far from the case. But it is true that cooking and catering by our members, especially at local agricultural shows, have always been a major source of fundraising, enabling the CWA to raise many hundreds of thousands of dollars over the years, which has been used to support families and communities particularly in rural areas.

The recipes in this series of cookbooks reflect the way in which our pioneer women used the simple ingredients they had to hand to make nutritious snacks, soups, stews, sweets and cakes, and would ensure their household a year-round supply of jams, jellies and relishes by preserving fruit when it was in season. Some of these recipes are family favourites and have been handed down through the generations, being adapted along the way to suit the available ingredients and local conditions. Many members have also adopted and adapted 'new' foods introduced to Australia from other countries.

We are proud to be working with Penguin Books in putting together these cookbooks and to be sharing with you our members' prized recipes. In so doing, once again CWA members are providing a valuable service to rural communities, as the royalties from the series (and from the recipe book Country Classics, which was republished by Penguin in 2007) will help us fund a postgraduate nursing scholarship. This is awarded to a nurse working in a rural area, allowing them to learn new skills and thus continue to provide an essential service to their community.

The scholarship is of especial importance as we see the nation's health services struggling – in all parts of Australia, but particularly in rural communities where sometimes the nurse is the only health professional available.

May you get as much pleasure from trying these recipes as the members of the Country Women's Association have in sharing them with you.

Lesley Young
National President (2006–2009)
Country Women's Association of Australia

About the CWA

The Country Women's Association was established in Australia during the early 1920s, in New South Wales. A conference was organised in Sydney in 1922 to coincide with the Easter Show, a time when many rural women 'came to town' with their families. There were increasing shared concerns about the issues facing women and their families in rural communities, and as well as agreeing on various social and political objectives the conference saw a committee formed to establish an organisation to promote the interests of women on the land. The idea was not new, as rural women's organisations had been around for many years in other parts of the world, the first recorded group having been formed in Finland in the 1700s.

Following the formation of this first CWA branch, many more spread throughout New South Wales and in other states. By the late 1930s there were CWA offices in all states and territories of Australia. During World War 2 the associations contributed in a number of ways to the war effort: local branches made their rooms and other facilities available and produced food, entertainment, equipment and clothing for Australian servicemen. They also helped the many women who were left behind to run the family farm while their husbands were away at the war.

In 1945 the state associations agreed to form a national body, the Country Women's Association of Australia. The first national meeting was held in Adelaide in 1946. Since those early days, our members have continued to support rural families and have lobbied governments on all sorts of matters including education, health, transport, aged care, child care and libraries. They have also addressed broader issues such as commodity prices, farm safety, GM crops, and water.

We are part of a world organisation of more than 9 million members in about 70 countries, the Associated Country Women of the World. The funds raised from our 'tea and scones' and other enterprises have allowed us to support many people in many different ways, not just in the country but throughout Australia and also overseas, including our sister members in the South Pacific.

At home, the range and scope of our activities have been of particular importance during the recent drought years, with money being donated from all levels of government and from corporations such as Woolworths (through their 'Drought Days' program), Bega Cheese and many others, for us to distribute to affected families. We have been able to pay families' emergency household expenses, have held community get-togethers, and have also supported other rural organisations. In addition to drought, some areas have experienced extreme and devastating rains and bushfires, and our branches have been able to assist, from their own emergency funds, those suffering hardship as a result.

Today we have some 44 000 members in 1855 branches country-wide. Even though our membership numbers are dwindling, I am confident that the Country Women's Association of Australia will continue to support rural communities for at least another 80 years. If you are interested in helping us with this work, we encourage you to join up – there will be a branch near you. Give your state office a call and see how you can become part of an organisation that cares for families not only in rural and remote areas but throughout Australia.

Raisin ring cake

JANET AVERY, LATROBE BRANCH, TAS.

125 g softened butter
1 cup caster sugar
2 eggs
1 cup sour cream
1 teaspoon vanilla essence
2 cups plain flour
1 teaspoon baking powder
1 teaspoon bicarbonate of soda
¼ teaspoon salt
½ cup raisins, chopped

topping

¼ cup sugar
½ cup chopped walnuts
½ cup chopped raisins
1 teaspoon mixed spice

SERVES 8–10

Preheat oven to 180°C. Grease a ring tin.

Cream butter and sugar until light and fluffy, then beat in eggs. Stir in sour cream and vanilla. Mix in sifted dry ingredients, then stir in raisins.

Spoon half the mixture into the prepared cake tin. Combine topping ingredients and sprinkle half over the batter. Spoon remaining cake mixture on top and sprinkle with remaining topping. Bake for 50–60 minutes. Cool for about 10 minutes before removing from the tin.

Black forest cheesecake

JOYCE GOOS, VALENTINE PLAINS BRANCH, QLD

crumb crust

250 g chocolate biscuits, crushed
110 g butter, melted

filling

230 g cream cheese
¾ cup sugar
1 tablespoon lemon juice
1 tablespoon gelatine
½ cup hot water
300 ml cream, whipped
1 × 425-g can cherries

topping

1 tablespoon arrowroot
1 tablespoon sugar
1 tablespoon rum (optional)

SERVES 10–12

Mix the crushed biscuits with the butter. Press into a 20-cm springform tin and refrigerate.

To make the filling, beat cream cheese with sugar and lemon juice. Dissolve gelatine in hot water and add to mixture. Fold in whipped cream, reserving some for decorating.

Drain cherries, saving the liquid. Pit cherries (if necessary) and cut each in half. Pour a third of the filling mixture into the crumb crust and arrange half the cherries on top. Pour on another third of the mixture and arrange remaining cherries on top. Pour remaining filling on top and refrigerate.

Combine reserved cherry liquid with arrowroot, sugar and rum (if desired) in a saucepan and bring to the boil. Remove from heat and cool slightly while stirring. Gently pour topping over cheesecake and use a knife to swirl it into the top centimetre of the filling mixture. Allow to set, then top with reserved whipped cream.

Lemony ginger cake

This recipe was often used on farms as a standby cake, as it uses only a few ingredients.

SHIRLEY TONGS, RANELAGH BRANCH, TAS.

125 g softened butter
1 cup sugar
1 egg
grated zest of 2 small lemons
2 cups plain flour
pinch of salt
2 teaspoons ground ginger
1 cup warm milk
1 teaspoon bicarbonate of soda
2 tablespoons golden syrup

SERVES 8–10

Preheat oven to 140°C. Grease a 20-cm × 11-cm loaf tin.

Beat butter and sugar to a light fluffy cream. Add egg and beat well. Add lemon zest. Sift flour with the salt and ginger. Combine warm milk with the bicarbonate of soda and golden syrup and add to the creamed mixture alternately with flour. Beat vigorously.

Pour into prepared tin and bake for about 1 hour (test after 45 minutes).

Sherry plain cake

My paternal grandfather started cooking sponge cakes for the Tucks Cake Shop in Launceston during the Depression. Later, my grandmother joined him, baking cakes both large and small. After the Second World War they were joined by their unmarried daughter, who helped to expand the business by making biscuits. This sherry plain cake was a particular favourite of mine, and I always asked to have it for my birthday.

BEV PERKINS, EAST LAUNCESTON BRANCH, TAS.

4 eggs
230 g sugar
230 g butter
230 g plain flour
2 tablespoons cornflour
½ teaspoon baking powder
pinch of salt
2 tablespoons sherry
1 tablespoon extra flour

SERVES 8

Preheat oven to 180°C. Grease and line a 20-cm square or round cake tin.

Beat eggs and sugar in a small bowl. In another bowl cream butter, add sifted flours, baking powder and salt, then beat in egg and sugar mixture. Add sherry and fold in the extra flour to prevent curdling.

Spoon mixture into prepared tin and bake for 45 minutes to 1 hour. When cold, top with icing made with sifted icing sugar, a little butter and some sherry.

Gourmet fruit cake

My family recipe originated in Ireland and England, and then travelled to America and Australia. Traditionally, it was cooked for Christmas, and was matured for as long as possible. My American cousin managed to keep one for 18 months and eventually cut the cake for her birthday – it had matured perfectly and tasted superb.

DAPHNE PLUMB, ESK BRANCH, QLD

- 450 g currants
- 340 g each of seedless raisins, seeded raisins, and dried figs, chopped
- 230 g dried prunes, cooked, drained, pitted and chopped
- 230 g dates, chopped
- 170 g glacé cherries, finely sliced
- 170 g candied citron, finely sliced
- 110 g candied orange peel, finely shredded
- 230 g almonds, blanched, toasted and slivered
- 3 cups dark rum (or whisky)
- 240 g softened butter
- 2 cups dark brown sugar
- 1½ teaspoons each of ground cinnamon, ground nutmeg, ground allspice
- 5 large eggs
- 2 cups plain flour
- 2 teaspoons baking powder
- ½ teaspoon salt

MAKES 2 CAKES (EACH SERVES 8–10)

Combine dried and candied fruit and almonds. Stir in rum (or whisky) and let the mixture stand for a week.

Preheat oven to 135°C. Butter two 8-cm deep 23-cm × 13-cm baking pans and line them with brown paper or baking paper, making sure the paper extends over the edge of the tins. Butter the paper lightly.

Cream butter and gradually blend in sugar and spices. Beat in 2 eggs. Sift together flour, baking powder and salt. Blend 1 cup of the flour mixture with the creamed mixture and beat in 3 more eggs. Stir in fruit and rum mixture and remaining flour, mixing the batter well.

Pour the batter into the prepared pans, pressing it down firmly into the corners, then drop filled pans from a height of 15 cm to eliminate any air bubbles. Place the cakes in the oven and put a shallow pan filled with hot water on the bottom of oven, underneath the cakes. Bake for 2½ hours, or until they test done. Cool the cakes in the pans for 1 hour, then transfer to wire racks, peel off the paper and leave to cool thoroughly.

Wrap cooled cakes in cheesecloth that has been soaked in rum and store in tightly covered containers. Let the cakes age as long as possible before serving (one month minimum), moistening cloths every month with dark rum.

Light fruit cake

HELEN WALL, CANIAMBO BRANCH, VIC.

1 × 300-ml can condensed milk

250 g butter

500 g mixed dried fruit (chopped apricots, apple and sultanas, or fruit medley)

2 cups plain flour

½ teaspoon bicarbonate of soda

½ teaspoon salt

SERVES 8

Preheat oven to 180°C. Grease and line a 20-cm cake tin.

Put condensed milk, 1¼ cups water, butter and fruit in a saucepan and stir over low heat until combined and butter is melted. Set aside for 10 minutes.

Sift flour, soda and salt into a bowl, then add to the fruit mixture and mix well.

Place mixture in the prepared tin and bake for 1¼ to 1½ hours.

Sweet potato fruit cake

GWYNETH WATKINS, GEORGE TOWN BRANCH, TAS.

¾ cup butter
2 tablespoons golden syrup
1 cup sugar
500 g mixed dried fruit
2 eggs, well beaten
1 cup mashed sweet potato
1 cup plain flour
1 cup self-raising flour
1 teaspoon mixed spice
1 teaspoon ground nutmeg
pinch of salt

SERVES 10–12

Preheat oven to 180°C. Grease a 22-cm square cake tin.

Melt butter in a large saucepan. Add golden syrup, sugar and mixed fruit and stir until sugar is dissolved. Remove from heat and add the eggs and sweet potato. When cool, add sifted flours, spices and salt.

Place in prepared tin and bake for 1½ hours.

Easy fruit cake

This cake makes a good wedding or Christmas cake. It should be kept for 6 to 12 months before serving.

MRS ANNETTE FERGUSSON, ORIELTON BRANCH, TAS.

- 750 g mixed dried fruit
- 250 g sultanas
- 125 g currants
- 125 g raisins
- 60 g mixed peel
- 60 g dates, chopped
- 100 g glacé cherries
- ½ cup whisky, rum, sherry or brandy
- 1 granny smith apple
- 1 tablespoon honey
- 1 cup firmly packed soft brown sugar
- 4 eggs
- 1½ cups plain flour
- ½ cup self-raising flour
- 1 teaspoon mixed spice
- ¼ teaspoon ground cinnamon
- ¼ teaspoon ground nutmeg
- 250 g butter, melted
- almonds and glacé cherries, for decorating
- 2 tablespoons extra whisky, rum, sherry or brandy

SERVES 14–16

Preheat oven to 150°C. Grease a deep 23-cm square cake tin and line it with three sheets of greaseproof paper, allowing the paper to come 5 cm above the edge of the tin.

Chop all dried fruit to about the size of sultanas. Place in a large bowl and add whisky. Leave to soak for several hours, or stand overnight if desired.

Add peeled and coarsely grated apple to the fruit mixture, along with the honey, sugar and eggs. Mix well with a wooden spoon or your hands, to break up any clumps of fruit. Sift flours and spices together and add to the fruit mixture with the cooled melted butter. Mix thoroughly.

Place mixture in prepared tin and decorate the top with almonds and cherries. Bake for 3½ hours, or until cooked when tested with a skewer. Remove from oven and brush top with extra whisky. Immediately cover the tin with foil, then leave until cold. Remove from tin, leaving lining paper intact. Seal in a plastic bag or wrap in cling wrap and refrigerate for at least 6 months before serving.

Coffee fruit cake

This is a lovely moist rich cake and it keeps well.

VAL TITLEY, KING ISLAND PEGARAH BRANCH, TAS.

1 kg mixed dried fruit
2 cups strong black coffee
1 × 150-g block fruit and nut chocolate, chopped
2 cups self-raising flour
icing sugar, to serve

SERVES 14–16

Preheat oven to 170°C. Grease a 5-cm deep 20-cm × 27-cm pan.

Place the dried fruit in a bowl and pour the coffee over. Leave to soak overnight.

The next day, combine fruit mixture with chocolate and sifted flour.

Place mixture in prepared pan. Bake for 1½ hours, or until cooked when tested. Dust with icing sugar before serving.

CLEMATIS

Pineapple fruit cake

BEVERLEY J. PRINS, GEORGE TOWN BRANCH, TAS.

1 × 440-g can pineapple pieces
500 g mixed dried fruit
125 g butter
1 large cup sugar
1 teaspoon mixed spice
1 teaspoon bicarbonate of soda
2 eggs, beaten
1 cup plain flour
1 cup self-raising flour

SERVES 14–16

Preheat oven to 180°C. Grease a deep 23-cm square or round cake tin.

Put undrained pineapple, dried fruit, butter, sugar, mixed spice and bicarbonate of soda into a saucepan. Stir over medium heat until mixture comes to the boil. Cool until cold, then add eggs and sifted flours. Mix well.

Pour into prepared cake tin and bake for 1½ to 2 hours.

Rich fruit cake

I have been using this recipe for many years for special occasion cakes, including for birthdays, engagements and weddings. The cake will keep for many months and improves in flavour on keeping.

MARION SPAULDING, HIGHCROFT/STORMLEA BRANCH, TAS.

500 g sultanas
500 g currants
500 g raisins
100 g mixed peel (optional)
100 g almonds
100 g glacé cherries
2 teaspoons mixed spice
2 teaspoons ground ginger
2 teaspoons ground cinnamon
2 teaspoons ground nutmeg
6 tablespoons sweet sherry
500 g softened butter
500 g soft brown sugar (or use dark brown sugar for a richer cake)
1 dozen medium eggs
500 g plain flour
100 g self-raising flour

MAKES 1 LARGE OR 2 SMALL CAKES (SERVES 12–16)

Chop up the dried fruit, nuts and cherries and mix with the spices and sherry. Leave to soak overnight.

Preheat oven to 150°C. Line one 25-cm cake tin or two 15-cm tins with baking paper, allowing the paper to come up over the sides.

Cream butter and sugar (preferably using your clean hands, instead of a spoon). Add eggs one at a time and beat well. Add half the fruit mixture and mix. Sift the flours together, then add half to the mixture and stir. Mix in remaining fruit, then add remaining flour and mix.

Fill the tin/s about three-quarters full, then bump them on the floor or kitchen bench to level the top and to disperse any air pockets. Bake in the preheated oven for 1½ hours, then reduce heat to 100°C and cook for a further 1½ hours, or until cooked when tested with a skewer. (I always place my cakes on 6–8 thicknesses of newspaper in the oven, to prevent overcooking on the bottom.)

Remove from oven, cover and allow to cool slowly. Turn out and wrap in cling wrap or newspaper until ready to use. Ice before serving if desired.

Favourite family fruit cake

This cake has been a favourite in the family for years – everyone makes it, and it tastes a bit different every time. You can make it with sultanas instead of the mixed fruit, or it is very nice as a plain cake (just omit the fruit and cook for a little less time).

M. M. STACKHOUSE, YARRAM BRANCH, VIC.

500 g softened butter
1 good cup sugar
4 eggs
500 g plain flour
½ teaspoon cream of tartar
¼ teaspoon bicarbonate of soda
375 g dried fruit (mixture of sultanas, currants, mixed peel or own selection)
1 teaspoon vanilla or almond essence

SERVES 12–14

Preheat oven to 180°C. Grease and line a 23-cm round cake tin.

Cream butter and sugar, then add eggs one at a time, beating well between each egg. Sift together flour and risings. Add a tablespoon of flour to the fruit and stir to coat. Then stir fruit and remaining flour into butter mixture. Add vanilla or almond essence and mix well.

Place mixture in prepared tin and bake for 1 to 1½ hours. This cake keeps very well.

Dried apricot and sultana log

NOELA MACLEOD, ESSENDON BRANCH, VIC.

1 cup boiling water
1 cup chopped dried apricots
1 cup sultanas
100 g softened butter
¾ cup sugar
1 egg
2 cups self-raising flour

SERVES 8–10

Preheat oven to 180–200°C. Grease a log tin or two small fruit tins.

Pour boiling water over apricots and sultanas, then set aside to cool.

Cream butter and sugar, beat in egg, then add sifted flour and cold fruit mixture.

Pour mixture into the prepared tin/s and bake in the oven for 30–35 minutes. When cold, slice and butter.

Potato kuchen cake

JOYCE GOOS, VALENTINE PLAINS BRANCH, QLD

2 tablespoons softened butter
½ cup warm mashed potato
1 cup sugar
¾ cup milk
vanilla extract, to taste
½ cup sultanas
½ teaspoon ground nutmeg
2 cups self-raising flour

topping
1 cup plain flour
1 cup sugar
55 g butter
1 teaspoon ground cinnamon

SERVES 8–10

Preheat the oven to 180°C (not fan-forced). Grease a 20-cm square tin or 28-cm × 20-cm tray.

Beat together butter, mashed potato, sugar, milk and vanilla. Add sultanas, nutmeg and sifted flour. Mix well. Pour mixture into prepared tin.

To make the topping, mix sifted flour with other ingredients until moist lumps form. Sprinkle topping evenly over cake mixture. Bake for approximately 30 minutes. This cake keeps for 2 days.

Lime cake

For a change, use a lemon or orange instead of the lime.

GWYNETH WATKINS, GEORGE TOWN BRANCH, TAS.

180 g softened butter
1 cup sugar
finely grated zest of 1 lime
2 eggs, lightly beaten
1¼ cups self-raising flour
⅓ cup almond meal
¾ cup sour cream
2 tablespoons lime juice
cream, to serve

SERVES 8

Preheat oven to 160°C. Lightly grease and line an 18-cm square cake tin.

Cream butter and sugar. Beat in zest and eggs. Fold in sifted flour, almond meal, sour cream and lime juice. Spread into prepared tin and bake for 1 hour.

Allow to cool slightly, then cut into squares and serve with a dollop of cream and a few shreds of lime zest.

Blueberry cake

JANET AVERY, LATROBE BRANCH, TAS.

¼ cup butter
¾ cup sugar
1 egg
zest of 1 lemon
⅓ cup yoghurt mixed with
1 teaspoon lemon juice
1½ cups plain flour
2 teaspoons baking powder
salt
2 cups blueberries

glaze

2 teaspoons softened butter
¼ cup sugar
1 tablespoon lemon juice

SERVES 8–10

Preheat oven to 180°C. Grease a 20-cm cake tin.

Place butter, sugar, egg and lemon zest in a food processor and blend briefly. Add yoghurt mixture, and sifted flour, baking powder and salt. Pulse a few times. Stir in blueberries.

Spread batter in prepared pan and bake in the preheated oven for 40–45 minutes. While it is cooking, make the glaze by heating all ingredients over low heat until sugar has dissolved. Brush the glaze over the cake just before it is done.

Gingerbread 1

I can remember my mother making this when I was a young child, and making it myself when I was old enough to make cakes. We used to beat it by hand in those days.

JUDY PRATT, DARWIN BRANCH, NT

- ½ cup margarine
- ½ cup sugar
- 1 egg
- a little less than 1 cup golden syrup
- 2 cups self-raising flour
- 1 teaspoon ground cinnamon
- 1 teaspoon ground ginger
- 1 cup hot water

SERVES 8–12

Preheat oven to 180°C. Grease and line a lamington tray – the baking paper should come up a little higher than the sides of the tray.

Cream margarine and sugar. Add egg and golden syrup and beat well. Add sifted flour, cinnamon and ginger together with hot water and beat until smooth and runny. Bake in prepared tray for 45 minutes.

Ice or butter when cool.

Gingerbread 2

This recipe was made for one of the Darwin Branch's conferences.

MARGARET McDERMID, DARWIN BRANCH, NT

1½ cups plain flour
1 cup self-raising flour
1 teaspoon bicarbonate of soda
2 teaspoons ground ginger
½ teaspoon ground cinnamon
½ teaspoon mixed spice
pinch of salt
1 cup sugar
2 eggs
1 cup milk
125 g butter
1 cup treacle

SERVES 10–14

Preheat oven to 180°C. Grease a 20-cm square cake tin.

Sift together the flours, bicarbonate of soda, spices and salt. Mix in the sugar, eggs and milk. In a small saucepan, heat the butter and treacle until butter is melted, then add to the flour mixture.

Pour batter into prepared tin and bake for 1 to 1½ hours. Cool in the tin for 10 minutes before turning out.

Feather patty cakes

These little cakes are feather-light.

JOYCE GOOS, VALENTINE PLAINS BRANCH, QLD

2 large tablespoons softened butter

1 cup sugar

vanilla essence, to taste

2 eggs

2 cups self-raising flour

¾ cup milk

MAKES 18

Preheat the oven to 180°C. Line two muffin pans with patty cases.

Cream butter, sugar and vanilla. Beat in eggs. Sift in flour and add milk. Mix well.

Place mixture into patty cases and bake for 30 minutes.

Pineapple carrot cake

EILEEN McMULLEN, RANELAGH BRANCH, TAS.

¾ cup plain flour
¾ cup self-raising flour
½ teaspoon ground cinnamon
½ teaspoon bicarbonate of soda
½ teaspoon salt
¾ cup caster sugar
1 cup finely grated carrot
2 eggs, beaten
1 × 450-g can crushed pineapple
½ cup vegetable oil

MAKES 2 CAKES
(EACH SERVES 8–10)

Preheat the oven to 180°C. Grease two 25-cm × 8-cm bar tins.

Sift the dry ingredients together, then add all other ingredients and mix well.

Pour into prepared tins. Bake for 45 minutes, or until cooked.

Rock cakes

JOYCE LOCKWOOD, GEORGE TOWN BRANCH, TAS.

3 cups self-raising flour
½ cup margarine
1½ cups sugar
3 eggs (add 1 extra if needed)
ground cinnamon, to taste
3 cups sultanas
2 teaspoons vanilla essence

MAKES 3 TRAYS (ABOUT 30)

Preheat oven to 200°C. Grease three baking trays.

Sift flour, then mix with all remaining ingredients.

Place spoonfuls of mixture on prepared baking trays. Bake for 15 to 30 minutes.

Cinnamon bun

This is my mum's recipe.

MRS ANNETTE FERGUSSON, ORIELTON BRANCH, TAS.

1 cup self-raising flour
1 teaspoon mixed spice
1 teaspoon ground cinnamon
2 tablespoons sugar
½ cup mixed dried fruit
30 g butter
½ cup milk
1 egg, beaten

topping

melted butter
ground cinnamon
sugar

SERVES 8

Preheat oven to 180°C. Grease a 5-cm deep 25-cm × 8-cm bar tin.

Sift the flour and spices together, then add the sugar and fruit. Melt the butter and combine with the milk. Add milk mixture and egg to the dry ingredients.

Pour mixture into prepared cake tin. Bake for 20 minutes. Remove from oven and while still hot spread melted butter on top and sprinkle with a mixture of cinnamon and sugar.

Slice and spread with butter to serve.

Ginger cake

NOELA MACLEOD, ESSENDON BRANCH, VIC.

250 g softened butter
1 cup sugar
1 cup golden syrup
3 eggs
3 cups plain flour
½ teaspoon salt
2 teaspoons ground ginger
2 teaspoons mixed spice
1 teaspoon ground cinnamon
1 teaspoon bicarbonate of soda
2 tablespoons boiling water
¼ cup chopped glacé ginger

SERVES 8–10

Preheat oven to 180°C. Grease a 20-cm square cake tin.

Cream the butter and sugar with the golden syrup. Add the eggs, one at a time, beating well after each addition. Add the sifted flour and salt and mix. Next add the spices. Dissolve the carb soda in the boiling water and add to the mixture. Stir in the glacé ginger and 1 cup water.

Place mixture in the prepared cake tin and bake in the oven for 30–40 minutes, until cooked.

Toni Brown's sponge

ELAINE YOUD, DEVONPORT BRANCH, TAS.

4 eggs
¾ cup caster sugar
1 cup cornflour
½ teaspoon bicarbonate of soda
1 teaspoon cream of tartar
whipped cream, to serve

SERVES 8

Preheat oven to 175°C. Grease two 20-cm round sponge tins.

Whip eggs with the caster sugar until thick and creamy (approximately 8–10 minutes). Using a wooden spoon, fold in the sifted cornflour, bicarbonate of soda and cream of tartar.

Pour into prepared tins and bake for 20 minutes. Fill with whipped cream.

Selma's moist sponge

Each time I arrived home from hospital after having one of my four children, I would find that my friend Selma had left this sponge cake for me on the kitchen table. The cake would be iced and filled with cream and jam, and next to it would be a homemade casserole and a flower for me to have as a keepsake. From a lovely friend, this recipe is handed down to my children.

ERIN MORRISON, STRAHAN BRANCH, TAS.

1 walnut-sized piece of butter
3 tablespoons milk
3 eggs
¾ cup caster sugar
not-quite-1-cup self-raising flour

SERVES 8

Preheat oven to 175°C. Grease two 20-cm cake tins.

Boil butter and milk in a saucepan. Cream eggs and sugar, then add sifted flour and butter mixture. Mix well.

Spoon into prepared pans and cook for 15–20 minutes.

Sponge cake

My mother won prizes at local shows with this cake many years ago. She made it quite often when I was growing up and it was enjoyed by our family and visitors alike. Incidentally, she would beat the eggs by hand those days.

A J KAPERNICK, CLOYNA BRANCH, QLD

4 eggs
¾ cup sugar
1 dessertspoon arrowroot
¾ cup self-raising flour
1 dessertspoon butter
4 dessertspoons boiling water
jam and icing sugar, or mock cream (page 179), to serve

SERVES 8–10

Preheat oven to 180°C. Grease two 20-cm sandwich tins.

Break eggs into a bowl and beat for 5 minutes. Add sugar gradually, beating well after each addition. Add the arrowroot to the flour and sift gently into the mixture a little at a time. Melt butter in the boiling water and pour into the mixture slowly, while continuing to mix.

Pour mixture into prepared tins and bake for about 20 minutes. Join the cooled cakes with jam and sprinkle the top with icing sugar, or if you prefer spread with mock cream.

Never-miss sponge cake

At a country wedding long ago – could it be 20 years? – everybody contributed their most successful cakes. I happened to be sitting next to one of the bride's aunts, and when I tasted a particularly delicious piece of cake, I simply had to tell her 'I wonder who made this scrumptious morsel?' 'I did,' was the answer, 'would you like the recipe?' She gave it to me there and then. I used it for ever after! All my friends make it. They called it 'The never-miss sponge cake'.

LOUISE DE GROOT, GEORGE TOWN BRANCH, TAS.

4 eggs
¾ cup caster sugar
½ cup self-raising flour
½ cup cornflour
¼ teaspoon cream of tartar
¼ teaspoon bicarbonate of soda
½ teaspoon vanilla essence

SERVES 10–14

Preheat oven to 230°C. Grease a 23-cm or 24-cm round cake tin.

Beat eggs, adding caster sugar gradually, until stiff. Sift flours with cream of tartar and bicarb soda. Add sifted ingredients to egg mixture all at once, stirring with a knife to keep it fluffy.

Pour mixture into prepared tin. Bake for 25 minutes, or until a skewer inserted into the centre comes out clean.

Banana cake with lemon cream-cheese frosting

CARMA STUDLEY, METROPOLITAN BRANCH, TAS.

110 g softened butter
110 g caster sugar
2 eggs
3 medium bananas, mashed
230 g self-raising flour
2 teaspoons bicarbonate of soda
⅓ cup milk

frosting

1 × 60-g packet cream cheese
30 g softened butter
1 teaspoon grated lemon zest
1½ cups icing sugar

SERVES 12–14

Preheat oven to 205°C. Grease a 28-cm × 18-cm slab tin or a 20-cm square cake tin.

Cream butter, add sugar and beat, then add eggs one at a time, creaming thoroughly. Fold in the mashed banana, then fold in the sifted flour alternately with the combined soda and milk.

Place mixture into the prepared cake tin and bake for approximately 30 minutes. When cake is cold, ice with cream-cheese frosting.

To make the frosting, beat the cream cheese, butter and zest in a small bowl until light and fluffy, then gradually beat in sifted icing sugar.

Chocolate banana cake

This is my daughter Rebecca's recipe.

ELAINE YOUD, DEVONPORT BRANCH, TAS.

2 cups plain flour
2 teaspoons baking powder
125 g softened unsalted butter
1 cup caster sugar
4 ripe bananas, mashed
2 eggs, lightly beaten
1 teaspoon vanilla essence
1 cup chocolate chips

SERVES 8–10

Preheat oven to 180°C. Lightly grease a loaf tin (or use a non-stick tin).

Sift flour and baking powder into a large bowl. In a separate bowl, beat the butter, sugar, mashed banana, eggs, vanilla and choc chips. Add to the dry ingredients and stir to combine. Do not overmix.

Pour batter into prepared tin and bake for 1¼ hours, or until cooked. Leave to cool in the tin for 5 minutes before turning out onto a wire rack. Serve in thick slices, spread with butter.

Moist banana cake

NOELA MACLEOD, ESSENDON BRANCH, VIC.

250 g softened butter
1 cup caster sugar
2 tablespoons golden syrup
3 eggs, lightly beaten
3 ripe bananas, mashed
½ cup chopped pecan nuts
2 cups self-raising flour
2 teaspoons ground ginger
cream-cheese frosting (page 178) or lemon icing (page 179)

SERVES 8–12

Preheat oven to 180–200°C. Grease a 30-cm × 21-cm lamington tin.

Cream butter, sugar and golden syrup. Add eggs and mashed banana. Stir in nuts and sifted flour and ginger.

Place mixture in prepared tin and bake for 30–35 minutes. When cold, ice with cream-cheese frosting or lemon icing.

Rich wedding cake

My mother came out from England in 1927, as a very young lady. She was an excellent cook and raised a family of five on a farm hand's wage. She was well known for her Christmas cakes and this one was added to and perfected over the years. I have converted it to metric measurements.

SHIRLEY TONGS, RANELAGH BRANCH, TAS.

1 × 450-g can crushed pineapple
1 kg seeded raisins
1 kg sultanas
1 kg mixed dried fruit
½ cup orange juice
½ cup brandy
750 g softened butter
375 g white sugar
375 g soft brown sugar
375 g plain flour
3 teaspoons ground nutmeg
3 teaspoons mixed spice
3 teaspoons baking powder
1 dozen eggs

MAKES 2 CAKES
(EACH SERVES 14)

Drain crushed pineapple, reserving ½ cup of the juice. Place the dried fruits and pineapple in a large bowl and add the orange juice, reserved pineapple juice and brandy. Leave overnight to allow the flavours to mix in.

Line two 18-cm × 26-cm tins with many layers of greased baking paper (the better your lining, the more evenly cooked your cake will be).

Cream butter and sugars in a large bowl. Sift together flour, spices and baking powder. Add eggs to the creamed mixture one at a time, alternately with the flour and fruit mixtures. Mix thoroughly (you may need to use your hands).

Add mixture to prepared tins. Slightly hollow out the centre top of each, so that as the cake cooks it won't crack. Bang the tins on the bench to help remove air pockets. Place in a cold oven and lay a piece of brown paper on top of each tin, so the cakes don't brown too much. Set oven at 150°C and bake for 1 hour, then reduce heat to 100°C and cook for about another 3 hours (time depends on your oven). Leave in the tins after removing from oven, until cooled. It's best to wrap the cakes in foil once cold. (You can pour brandy over the cold cakes before wrapping if you want to keep them for a long time.)

Mum's orange tea cake

My mum made this cake often when our orange trees had lots of fruit. It was a favourite with the workers on our farm, and she always made double the recipe so that there would be some left for us after school.

FAY CAWTHRAY (NEE GENN), MIRIAM VALE/BOROREN BRANCH, QLD

2 rounded tablespoons softened butter
½ cup sugar
1 egg, beaten
zest and juice of 1 orange
1 cup self-raising flour
1 dessertspoon cornflour
milk, if needed
1 tablespoon extra sugar

SERVES 8

Preheat oven to 180°C. Grease a round 20-cm cake tin and line the base with paper.

Cream butter and sugar, add egg and beat well. Add zest and juice of orange (mixture will curdle). Sift in the dry ingredients and mix well. If there's not enough juice in the orange, a little milk may be added.

Pour into prepared tin and sprinkle with extra sugar. Bake for about 30 minutes, until cooked.

This is great for smokos, served sliced and buttered.

Peach, almond and yoghurt cake

This recipe is the most used in my kitchen.

MELISSA ANICTOMATIS, PORT DARWIN BRANCH, NT

- 220 g softened unsalted butter
- 250 g caster sugar
- 1 teaspoon vanilla extract
- 3 eggs
- 300 g self-raising flour, sifted
- 50 ml milk
- 250 g natural yoghurt
- 1 teaspoon amaretto, or other liqueur (optional)
- 450 g small fresh peaches, peeled, stoned and chopped (or use tinned)
- 50 g flaked almonds
- ½ cup extra natural yoghurt
- ½ cup cream

SERVES 10–12

Preheat oven to 170°C. Grease a 23-cm springform tin and line the base with non-stick baking paper.

Cream the butter and sugar until light and fluffy. Add vanilla, then add eggs one at a time, beating well after each addition. Add half the sifted flour, the milk, and half the yoghurt, and beat for about a minute. Add remaining flour and yoghurt, along with the liqueur (if using) and mix. Fold in the chopped peaches.

Pour mixture into the prepared tin and scatter almonds on top. Bake for 1½ hours or until cooked. (If you find the cake is browning too quickly, cover with some aluminium foil.) Remove from the oven and leave in the tin to cool.

Place the extra yoghurt and cream in a bowl and beat until thick. Serve on the side.

Rhubarb coconut cake

PHYLLIS HINGSTON, SASSAFRAS/WESLEY VALE BRANCH, TAS.

- 1½ cups self-raising flour
- 1¼ cups caster sugar
- 1¼ cups desiccated coconut
- 125 g butter, melted
- 3 eggs, lightly beaten
- ½ cup milk
- ½ teaspoon vanilla essence
- ¾ cup (about 90 g) finely chopped rhubarb
- 2 stalks extra rhubarb, cut into 5-cm lengths
- 2 tablespoons soft brown sugar

SERVES 10–12

Preheat oven to 180°C. Grease a deep 20-cm round cake tin and line the base with baking paper.

Combine sifted flour with the caster sugar and coconut in a bowl. Stir in the melted butter, eggs, milk and vanilla. Spread half the cake mixture into the prepared tin, then scatter chopped rhubarb evenly over the top. Spread remaining cake mixture over the rhubarb, then arrange extra rhubarb pieces over the top of the cake. Sprinkle with the soft brown sugar.

Bake for 1 hour. Leave to cool in the tin for 5 minutes before turning out onto a wire rack. (This cake is suitable to freeze.)

Enjoy!

Boiled plum pudding

JOYCE GOOS, VALENTINE PLAINS BRANCH, QLD

2½ cups plain flour
1 cup sugar
3 cups mixed dried fruit
1 teaspoon mixed spice
1 teaspoon ground cinnamon
1 teaspoon ground nutmeg
1 teaspoon ground ginger
2 teaspoons bicarbonate of soda
1 cup boiling water
2 tablespoons butter
2 tablespoons golden syrup
¼ cup rum (optional)

SERVES 12

Sift flour into a basin and stir in sugar, fruit and spices. Dissolve the bicarbonate of soda in 1 cup cold water and add to the fruit mixture. Dissolve butter and golden syrup in the boiling water, add to the batter and mix well. Stir in rum (if using). Cover and leave overnight.

The next day, remix batter and pour into a pudding cloth that has been dipped into boiling water. Tie securely and boil in a large pan of boiling water for 4 hours (be careful not to boil dry).

Five-minute orange cake

This recipe was forwarded to me from Adelaide. It is such a wonderful moist cake that I have consequently handed it to all my friends in Darwin.

WENDY WHITE, DARWIN BRANCH, NT

1 × 200-g navel orange (I make sure I weigh the orange, as if it is too large it will make the cake overly moist)

175 g butter, chopped (at room temperature)

3 eggs

1 cup caster sugar

2 cups self-raising flour

icing

60 g softened butter

2 teaspoons grated orange zest

2 tablespoons orange juice

2 cups icing mixture

SERVES 10–12

Preheat oven to 180°C. Thoroughly grease a 22-cm baba pan with butter.

Cut the unpeeled orange into segments, remove pips and place in a food processor. Process until finely chopped. Add chopped butter, eggs, sugar and sifted flour and process until well combined.

Spread mixture in prepared pan and bake for about 45 minutes, or until cooked when tested. Stand the cake in the pan for 5 minutes before turning out onto a wire rack to cool.

To make the orange icing, beat the butter and zest (I use the Mix Master), then gradually add the juice and sifted icing sugar.

(This cake can also be made in a lined 22-cm round cake pan. Cook for about 1 hour, covering the cake lightly with a piece of aluminium foil to prevent it from over-browning.)

Walnut coffee cake

This is a Sunday-night special.

ELAINE YOUD, DEVONPORT BRANCH, TAS.

2 tablespoons softened butter
⅓ cup sugar
1 egg, beaten
½ teaspoon vanilla essence
pinch of salt
1 cup self-raising flour
½ cup milk

filling/topping

2 tablespoons softened butter
½ cup soft brown sugar
2 tablespoons self-raising flour
½ teaspoon ground cinnamon
½ cup chopped walnuts
½ cup desiccated coconut

SERVES 8

Preheat oven to 170–180°C. Grease a 20-cm sandwich tin.

Cream butter and sugar, add beaten egg, vanilla essence and salt and beat. Fold in sifted flour and add milk. Stir to combine.

To make filling/topping, cream butter and sugar, then add sifted flour and cinnamon. Stir in the walnuts and coconut.

Spread half the cake mixture in the prepared tin, then spread over half the filling, then remaining cake mixture and lastly remaining filling.

Bake for 20 minutes.

Hawaiian tea cake

I received this recipe from my mother, Alma Winning (Theodore Branch, Qld).

LINDY CLEELAND, ORIELTON BRANCH, TAS.

¼ cup softened butter
¼ cup sugar
1 egg, well beaten
1 cup self-raising flour
pinch of salt
2 tablespoons milk
½ cup well-drained pineapple

topping

2 teaspoons butter, melted
2 teaspoons ground cinnamon
2 teaspoons sugar

SERVES 8

Preheat oven to 180°C. Grease a 20-cm sandwich tin.

Cream butter and sugar, then gradually add the egg. Sift flour and salt and add to the creamed mixture alternately with the milk.

Spread mixture in prepared tin and arrange pineapple on top.

Bake for approximately 20 minutes. When cooked, brush with melted butter and sprinkle with the combined cinnamon and sugar.

Christmas cake for dieters

NOELA MACLEOD, ESSENDON BRANCH, VIC.

1 cup currants
1 cup raisins
1 cup sultanas
½ cup glacé cherries
½ cup mixed peel
¼ teaspoon ground ginger
¼ teaspoon ground nutmeg
1 teaspoon ground cinnamon
1 cup unsweetened fruit juice
2 cups self-raising flour
½ cup skim milk
1 egg

SERVES 8–10

Preheat oven to 180°C. Grease a 20-cm cake tin.

Place the fruit, spices and juice in a large saucepan. Stir over low heat until the mix is at a simmer. Simmer for 3 minutes, then remove from the heat and cool for at least 30 minutes (but do not allow the mix to become cold). Add the sifted flour, milk and egg. Blend, then pour mixture into prepared tin. Bake for 45 minutes.

Rich Christmas pudding

This pudding recipe has been handed down from generation to generation, and is more than 100 years old.

BEVERLEY LEE, CENTRAL COAST BRANCH, TAS.

450 g breadcrumbs
230 g plain flour
450 g butter
450 g soft brown sugar
3 small carrots, finely grated
3 small apples, finely grated
8 fresh eggs
1.8 kg mixed dried fruit, including a few dates
4 tablespoons treacle
360 ml brandy (or ale)
1 × 100-g packet glacé cherries
2 tablespoons marmalade (optional)
1 teaspoon ground cinnamon
1 teaspoon mixed spice
1 teaspoon ground ginger
1 teaspoon ground nutmeg

MAKES FOUR OR FIVE 1½-KG PUDDINGS (EACH SERVES 8–10)

Mix all ingredients together (you can add larger quantities of the spices if you like, but I don't like a lot of spice) and stand overnight.

Divide mixture into four or five portions and wrap each in cloth. Boil puddings for 4 to 5 hours, topping up water as necessary.

Ruth's Christmas cake

EILEEN McMULLEN, RANELAGH BRANCH, TAS.

1 kg mixed dried fruit
1 × 125-g packet glacé cherries
1 cup port wine
1 tablespoon golden syrup
1 cup soft brown sugar
4 large eggs
250 g butter, melted (can be added while still hot)
½ cup plain flour
½ cup self-raising flour
1 teaspoon mixed spice
2 teaspoons extra port (optional)

SERVES 8

Combine the dried fruit and cherries with the port wine and soak for 5 days at room temperature, stirring every day. (You can add extra port if necessary, but all liquid should be absorbed by the last day.)

On the fifth day, preheat the oven to 150°C. Grease and line a 20-cm square cake tin.

To the fruit mixture, add golden syrup, sugar, eggs, melted butter, and sifted flours and spice. Add the extra port if desired. Mix well.

Pour mixture into prepared tin and bake very slowly for 3–4 hours.

(Note: The mixture must be made up on the fifth day – don't let the fruit continue to ferment.)

Boiled chocolate cake

I have been cooking this family favourite for nearly forty years.

JOAN BEITZEL, FORREST BEACH BRANCH, NORTH QLD

170 g butter
1 cup white sugar
2 tablespoons cocoa
1 teaspoon bicarbonate of soda
1 teaspoon vanilla
2 eggs, lightly beaten
2 cups self-raising flour
pinch of salt
2 tablespoons sultanas or mixed dried fruit (optional)
a heaped teaspoon allspice (optional)
mock cream (page 179)
chocolate icing (page 176)

SERVES 8

Preheat oven to 170°C (fan-forced). Grease and line a 20-cm cake tin.

In a saucepan, combine butter, 1 cup water, sugar, cocoa and soda. Bring to the boil. Allow to cool, then add vanilla and eggs. Add sifted flour and salt and beat until smooth. Stir in sultanas and allspice (if using).

Pour into prepared tin and bake for 35–45 minutes, or until cooked. (This cake freezes well.)

To serve, slice through, fill with mock cream and top with chocolate icing.

(To make a jaffa chocolate cake, just substitute soft brown sugar for the white sugar, use ½ cup each of orange juice and water instead of all water, and leave out the vanilla.)

Kim's chocolate cake

KEREN McCALLUM, METROPOLITAN BRANCH, TAS.

2 cups self-raising flour
2 tablespoons cocoa
1½ cups sugar
1½ cups milk
2 eggs
2 tablespoons butter, melted

SERVES 8

Preheat oven to 180°C. Grease and line a 23-cm round cake tin.

Sift the flour and cocoa into a bowl. Add the sugar, milk and eggs. Beat with an electric mixer for 2 minutes. Add the melted butter and beat for another 2 minutes.

Pour into prepared tin and bake for about 1 hour.

Chocolate fudge cake

JANET AVERY, LATROBE BRANCH, TAS.

55 g softened butter

1 cup soft brown sugar

⅓ cup sour milk (milk with a little lemon juice added)

1 egg

1 cup self-raising flour

½ teaspoon bicarbonate of soda

2 tablespoons cocoa

SERVES 8

Preheat oven to 180°C. Grease a 20-cm cake tin.

Cream butter and sugar. Very gently add sour milk, watching that it doesn't curdle. Add egg and half of the sifted dry ingredients and beat for a few minutes, then mix in remaining flour mixture and beat for another minute.

Pour into prepared tin and bake for 30 minutes.

Grandma's chocolate cake

This is an excellent cake for lunches, it keeps well and is so versatile. You can use it to make muffins (makes 18 big muffins), or even steam it for a pudding. Other combinations of cake and pudding mixes can be used: e.g. vanilla cake mix and strawberry instant pudding.

JEAN BLACK, GLENELG BRANCH, VIC.

2 × packets chocolate cake mix
1 × packet chocolate pudding mix
4 eggs
1 cup water
½ cup vegetable oil
chocolate icing (page 176)
marshmallows, for decorating (optional)

SERVES 12–16

Preheat oven to 180°C. Grease a 25-cm square cake tin or a bunt tin.

Place all ingredients in a large mixing bowl and beat until creamy. Pour into prepared tin. Bake for 1 to 1½ hours (note that cooking in a bunt tin will take longer than in a 25-cm tin).

Once cool, ice with chocolate icing and decorate with small marshmallows if desired.

Never-fail chocolate cake

KATHRYN MUIR, TENNANT CREEK BRANCH, NT

2 cups self-raising flour
2 tablespoons cocoa
2 cups sugar
2 tablespoons instant coffee
4 eggs
½ cup Brandavino
180 g butter or margarine, melted
dash of vanilla essence

MAKES 1 LARGE OR 2 SMALL CAKES (SERVES 12–16)

Preheat oven to 180°C. Grease one 23-cm cake tin or two smaller tins.

Sift flour and cocoa into a bowl and combine with all other ingredients. Pour into prepared tin/s and bake for 45 minutes.

Serve plain or iced.

Moist chocolate cake

NOELA MACLEOD, ESSENDON BRANCH, VIC.

125 g dark cooking chocolate
250 g butter
1½ cups caster sugar
1½ cups lightly packed cold mashed potato
⅔ cup cocoa
4 eggs
3 cups self-raising flour
pinch of salt
⅔ cup milk

icing

90 g dark cooking chocolate, roughly chopped
1 teaspoon oil
2 cups icing sugar (approximately)

SERVES 8–12

Preheat oven to 180°C. Grease and line a 28-cm × 18-cm square tin.

To make the cake, melt the chocolate in the top of a double-boiler or in a small heat-proof basin set over a saucepan of simmering water. Set aside to cool.

Beat butter, then add sugar and potato and beat well. Add melted chocolate and sifted cocoa, then add eggs one at a time, beating well after each addition. Fold in sifted flour and salt alternately with milk.

Pour mixture into prepared tin and bake for about 1 hour. (The time may be more or less depending on your oven.) Cool on a wire rack. When cold, trim the top of cake with a sharp knife to level it, then place on a suitably covered decorative cake board.

To make the chocolate icing, combine chocolate, oil and 4 tablespoons water in the top of a double-boiler or in a basin set over simmering water. Stir until chocolate has melted. Remove from heat and gradually beat in sifted icing sugar, beating until smooth and of a good spreading consistency. Immediately spread the icing over the top and sides of the cooled cake, spreading it evenly and working quickly.

You can halve the recipe and bake in two sponge tins (bake for 30–35 minutes) then join the cakes together with whipped cream or raspberry jam before icing. Or to bake in a 25-cm tin, double the mixture and cook for 1¼–1½ hours.

Chocolate cake

WILMA DELL, DEVONPORT BRANCH, TAS.

2 cups self-raising flour
1½ cups sugar
1½ cups milk
2 eggs (unbeaten)
4 tablespoons cocoa
pinch of salt
2 tablespoons butter, melted
whipped cream
chocolate icing (page 176)
peppermint flavouring (optional)

SERVES 8

Preheat the oven to 180°C. Thoroughly grease a 20-cm square cake tin.

Sift flour into a bowl, then add sugar, milk, eggs, cocoa and salt and mix until smooth. Add butter and beat for another 2 minutes.

Pour into prepared tin and bake for 35 minutes. Once cool, fill with whipped cream and ice with chocolate icing. (A few drops of peppermint flavouring can be added to the icing.)

Pineapple cupcakes

JOYCE GOOS, VALENTINE PLAINS BRANCH, QLD

1 cup crushed Weet-Bix
¾ cup milk
pinch of bicarbonate of soda
55 g softened butter
55 g sugar
1 egg
2 tablespoons honey
½ cup drained crushed pineapple
2 cups plain flour
3 teaspoons baking powder

MAKES 24

Preheat oven to 180°C. Line two muffin pans with patty cases.

Place Weet-Bix in a basin, add milk and bicarbonate of soda. Stand aside. Cream butter and sugar. Stir in egg, honey and milky Weet-Bix. Stir in pineapple. Sift in flour and baking powder and mix well.

Place the mixture into patty cases and cook for about 20 minutes.

Never-fail pavlova

This recipe has been around the world. I've been making it for a restaurant for years. I use a free-standing mixer, but others have had success with a handheld electric beater.

BEVERLEY LEE, CENTRAL COAST BRANCH, TAS.

4 egg whites
1 tablespoon cornflour
1½ cups sugar
pinch of salt
5 tablespoons boiling water
1 good teaspoon vinegar
1 teaspoon vanilla essence

SERVES 8

Preheat fan-forced oven to 200°C. Line an oven tray with aluminium foil.

Place egg whites in a large bowl. Combine cornflour and sugar and add to the egg whites, then add a pinch of salt and the boiling water. Beat on high until the sugar has dissolved and the mixture holds its shape well – halfway through the beating add the vinegar and vanilla essence.

Pile the mixture onto the prepared oven tray and use a spatula to mould the mixture, until it is a bit larger than a cooked sponge cake.

Place in preheated oven, close the door, then turn the oven back to 1 stroke below 150°C. Bake for 1 hour. (Ovens will vary, so if the pav starts to tinge, turn the temperature back a little.)

Once cooked, turn the pav upside down onto a hot pav plate and carefully peel off the foil. The pav will keep for a few days before being decorated if need be. I think the best topping is whipped cream, sliced banana and black passionfruit.

Orange cake

JUNE WEAVER, GEORGE TOWN BRANCH, TAS.

125 g butter
1 cup sugar
2 eggs
½ cup milk
1½ cups self-raising flour
grated zest of 1 orange

SERVES 8–10

Preheat oven to 180°C. Grease a 20-cm cake tin.

Melt the butter, then add to a bowl with the sugar, eggs, milk, sifted flour and zest. Mix with an electric mixer on medium–high speed for 6 minutes.

Place in prepared cake tin. Bake for 30–45 minutes, depending on the size of the tin used. Test cake using the skewer method.

(You can decorate the cake with slices of candied orange peel if desired.)

Carrot cake

NOELA MACLEOD, ESSENDON BRANCH, VIC.

⅔ cup canola oil
⅓ cup soft brown sugar
2 eggs
½ cup honey
1 cup plain flour
¾ cup wholemeal plain flour
1 teaspoon mixed spice
1½ teaspoons baking powder
1 teaspoon bicarbonate of soda
2 cups grated carrot
½ cup chopped pecan nuts
½ cup chopped raisins
cream-cheese frosting (page 178)

SERVES 10–12

Preheat oven to 180°C. Grease a deep 20-cm square cake tin and line it with greased greaseproof paper.

Place oil, brown sugar, eggs and honey into a bowl and beat until thick and creamy. Sift together flours, spice, baking powder and carb soda, tipping any husks from the sifter back into the flour. Fold flours into oil mixture alternately with carrots, nuts and raisins.

Pour mixture into the prepared cake tin and bake for 55–60 minutes, until cake is cooked when tested. Stand in the tin for 5 minutes before turning out on to cooling tray.

When cool ice with cream-cheese frosting.

Malteser cake

SHIRLEY MORRISBY, BELLERIVE BRANCH, TAS.

1 cup self-raising flour

¾ cup caster sugar

4 tablespoons cocoa

2 eggs

2 tablespoons vegetable oil

2 × 150-g tubs Vanilla Crème Frûche

1 × 165-g packet Maltesers

SERVES 8

Preheat oven to 175°C. Grease an 18-cm square cake tin.

Sift together flour, sugar and cocoa. In a separate bowl combine eggs, oil and Frûche. Combine wet and dry ingredients, then stir through Maltesers.

Place mixture into the prepared cake tin and bake for 25–30 minutes.

Lemon coconut cake

This is my friend Barb Parson's special cake.

ELAINE YOUD, DEVONPORT BRANCH, TAS.

1½ cups self-raising flour
½ cup desiccated coconut
1 cup sugar
2 eggs
1 cup milk
125 g butter, melted
grated zest of 3 lemons

icing

1½ cups icing sugar
½ cup desiccated coconut
½ cup lemon juice

SERVES 8

Preheat oven to 160°C. Grease a 20-cm square cake tin.

Place sifted flour, coconut and sugar in a bowl and make a well in the centre. In a separate bowl, beat eggs, milk, melted butter and lemon zest. Pour egg mixture into the well in the dry ingredients and mix (the mixture will be quite sloppy).

Pour mixture into the prepared cake tin and bake for 45–50 minutes.

To make icing, mix sifted icing sugar with coconut and lemon juice. Ice the cake once it is cold.

Black forest torte

JANET AVERY, LATROBE BRANCH, TAS.

½ cup caster sugar
3 eggs, separated
1 golden delicious apple, grated
¾ cup cashews, chopped
⅓ cup breadcrumbs

topping

400 ml cream
1 × 425-g can black cherries, drained
chocolate flakes

SERVES 8–10

Preheat the oven to 180°C. Grease a 20-cm springform cake tin.

Beat sugar and egg yolks, then fold in apple, nuts and breadcrumbs. Whip egg whites until stiff peaks form, then fold into the batter. Place mixture in prepared tin and bake for about 45 minutes.

For the topping, whip cream and spread most of it over the top and sides of the cake. Pipe lines of cream across the top of the cake, to create sections, then fill these sections with cherries and sprinkle with chocolate flakes.

Lemon delicious pudding

JOYCE GOOS, VALENTINE PLAINS BRANCH, QLD

1 tablespoon softened butter
1 cup sugar
2 tablespoons self-raising flour
juice of 2 lemons
1 cup milk
2 eggs, separated
custard (page 178)

SERVES 3–4

Preheat oven to 150°C (not fan-forced). Grease a 1-litre casserole dish.

In the casserole dish, cream the butter and sugar. Add sifted flour, lemon juice, milk, and lightly beaten egg yolks. Mix well. Lastly, add the stiffly beaten egg whites.

Place in the oven and bake for about 25–30 minutes. When cooked, the pudding will be cake-like on top, with lemon filling underneath.

Serve with custard.

Custard cake

JOAN BEITZEL, FORREST BEACH BRANCH, NORTH QLD

110 g butter
⅓ cup sugar
1 egg
¾ cup self-raising flour
¼ cup custard powder
icing sugar, to serve

custard

2 egg yolks, well beaten
1 cup milk
2 tablespoons sugar
2 tablespoons custard powder
1 teaspoon vanilla essence

SERVES 8

Make custard first. Beat egg yolks with some of the milk, then heat the remaining milk and the sugar. Add egg mixture and custard powder to the milk and stir constantly over low heat until custard boils and thickens. Transfer to a container, cover with cling wrap to prevent a skin forming, and allow to cool to room temperature for easier spreading.

Preheat oven to 180°C. Grease an 18-cm sandwich tin and line the base and sides with greased baking paper.

For the cake, cream butter and sugar until light and fluffy, add egg, beat well, then add sifted flour and custard powder and beat until soft and smooth.

Spread half the cake mixture over the base of the prepared tin, cover with custard, then spread remaining cake mixture carefully on top. Bake for 35–40 minutes.

Dust with icing sugar before serving. This cake is delicious if eaten while still warm.

Pumpkin spice cake

NOELA MACLEOD, ESSENDON BRANCH, VIC.

500 g butter, chopped
1 cup caster sugar
½ cup firmly packed soft brown sugar
2 tablespoons grated orange zest
4 large eggs
1 cup sultanas
½ cup chopped raisins
½ cup currants
1 cup desiccated coconut
1 cup cold mashed pumpkin
4 cups self-raising flour
2 teaspoons ground cinnamon
1 teaspoon ground nutmeg
1 cup milk
3 tablespoons orange juice
cream-cheese frosting (page 178)

SERVES 14–16

Preheat oven to 160°C. Grease and line a 28-cm round cake tin.

Cream the butter, sugars and zest until creamy and fluffy. Add eggs one at a time, beating well after each addition. Stir in dried fruits, coconut and pumpkin. Mix in half the sifted flour and spices, half the milk, then mix in remaining flour and milk. Stir in orange juice.

Spread mixture into the prepared cake tin. Bake for about 1 hour 40 minutes, or until cooked. Leave in the tin for about 10 minutes before turning out onto a wire cooling rack. When cold, ice with cream-cheese frosting.

Mexican wedding cake

SHIRLEY MORRISBY, BELLERIVE BRANCH, TAS.

2 cups plain flour

1 × 450-g can crushed pineapple in natural juice

1½ cups sugar

2 eggs

2 teaspoons bicarbonate of soda

1 cup chopped walnuts

cream-cheese frosting

125 g cream cheese, at room temperature

60 g softened butter

½ cup icing sugar

½ teaspoon vanilla essence

SERVES 8–12

Preheat the oven to 180°C. Lightly grease a 28-cm × 18-cm lamington tin.

Sift flour, then combine with all other ingredients (except nuts). Stir in walnuts.

Pour into prepared tin and bake for 45 minutes. Once cake is cooled, spread with the cream cheese icing.

To make the frosting, mix all ingredients together until creamy.

Tea cake

HELEN WALL, CANIAMBO BRANCH, VIC.

1 egg, separated
½ cup sugar
½ cup milk
½ teaspoon vanilla
1 cup self-raising flour
1 tablespoon butter, melted

topping
melted butter
ground cinnamon
sugar

SERVES 8

Preheat oven to 180°C. Grease a 20-cm sandwich tin.

Beat egg white stiffly, whisk in sugar, then yolk. Stir in milk, vanilla, sifted flour and melted butter.

Pour into prepared tin and bake for 20–25 minutes. Remove from oven and while still hot brush with melted butter and sprinkle with a little cinnamon and sugar.

Date and nut loaf

JUDY PRATT, DARWIN BRANCH, NT

1 cup chopped dates
½ cup sugar
½ cup walnuts
1 tablespoon butter
1 teaspoon bicarbonate of soda
pinch of salt
1 cup boiling water
170 g self-raising flour

SERVES 8–10

Preheat oven to 180°C. Grease a loaf tin.

Place dates, sugar, walnuts, butter, soda and salt into basin. Add boiling water and allow to stand until mixture is cold. Then add sifted flour and mix well.

Pour into prepared tin and bake for 30–35 minutes. (Turn oven off about 10 minutes before cake is cooked.)

Serve sliced, with butter.

Sultana cake

As a young child, I lived with my mother at my grandparents' home during the war years, while my father was serving his country. I well remember sitting at the large table in the kitchen, watching fruit cakes and tarts being mixed by hand and biscuits being iced.

BEV PERKINS, EAST LAUNCESTON BRANCH, TAS.

450 g softened butter
450 g sugar
6 eggs
½ cup mixed peel
milk
3¾ cups plain flour
1 rounded teaspoon baking powder
680 g sultanas
almond essence, to taste
lemon essence, to taste (optional)

SERVES 12–16

Preheat oven to 150°C. Line a 25-cm cake tin.

Cream butter and sugar, then add eggs one at a time, beating well. Spoon the peel into a ½ cup measure, then fill the cup with milk. Add peel and milk to butter mixture and mix well. Sift together flour and baking powder, add to batter and mix. Stir in sultanas and essences.

Place mixture in prepared tin and cook for 2 hours.

CAKES

Apple kuchen

JANET AVERY, LATROBE BRANCH, TAS.

½ cup plain flour
2 teaspoons baking powder
salt
sugar or sweetener, to taste
¼ cup butter
½ cup yoghurt
2 eggs

topping

½ cup self-raising flour
⅓ cup sugar
3 tablespoons butter
2 medium apples, peeled and sliced

SERVES 14–16

Preheat oven to 175°C. Grease a 23-cm square baking pan.

To make streusel topping, place flour, sugar and butter in a food processor and process until crumbly. Transfer to a bowl and add apple slices, stirring to coat.

For the cake, add all ingredients to the food processor and process briefly. Scrape down the sides, then process for a few more seconds.

Spread batter in prepared pan. Neatly arrange the apple-streusel mixture on top. Bake for 40–45 minutes.

Irish apple cake

NOELA MACLEOD, ESSENDON BRANCH, VIC.

250 g plain flour

1 rounded teaspoon baking powder

125 g sugar

125 g butter

3–4 cooking apples, peeled, cored and roughly chopped

1 egg, beaten

⅓ cup milk

SERVES 8

Preheat oven to 180°C. Grease a 20-cm round cake tin.

Sift together the flour, baking powder and sugar. Cut in butter roughly (do not rub it in or cream it), then add the apples. Stir in egg and milk to make a fairly stiff mixture. (The batter will be fairly lumpy.)

Pour mixture into prepared tin and bake for about 1 hour. Serve hot, with custard, cream or ice-cream.

Apple cake

This recipe was handed down from my mother. She baked it for the workmen who helped out at our farm during shearing and harvest times. A basket of cakes and slices and a billy of tea were sent out at 9.45 a.m. and 3 p.m. and the basket always came back empty.

MARY HANSLOW, ORIELTON BRANCH, TAS.

110 g softened butter
½ cup sugar
1 egg
1 cup plain flour
1 teaspoon ground cinnamon
1 teaspoon ground ginger
1 teaspoon mixed spice
1 teaspoon cream of tartar
½ teaspoon bicarbonate of soda
milk
1 cup cold stewed apples

SERVES 8

Preheat the oven to 180°C. Thoroughly grease a 20-cm sandwich tin.

Cream the butter and sugar, add egg and beat well. Add the sifted flour, cinnamon, ginger, mixed spice, cream of tartar and bicarbonate of soda. Mix well and add a little milk if needed.

Place three-quarters of the mixture into the prepared sandwich tin, spread the stewed apple on top, then spread remaining mixture on top of the apple. Bake for about 40 minutes.

White chocolate mud cake

BEVERLEY LEE, CENTRAL COAST BRANCH, TAS.

250 g white cooking chocolate, chopped

250 g butter, chopped

200 ml hot water

1½ cups caster sugar

1¾ cups plain flour

1 cup self-raising flour

3 eggs, lightly beaten

1 teaspoon vanilla essence

frosting

100 g white cooking chocolate, chopped

¼ cup cream

250 g softened cream cheese (can be softened in the microwave for a few seconds)

SERVES 10–12

Preheat oven to 180°C. Grease a 22-cm round cake tin and line the base.

Combine chocolate, butter, water and sugar in a saucepan and place over medium heat. Stir continuously, until sugar has dissolved and chocolate has melted. Set aside to cool. Sift flours into a large bowl, add chocolate mixture, eggs and vanilla and mix well.

Place mixture into prepared tin. Bake for 1 to 1¼ hours or until cake is cooked (it should be golden on top). Leave in the tin to cool for about 20 minutes before turning out on to a wire rack.

To make frosting, stir chocolate and cream over low heat until chocolate is melted and smooth. Allow to cool a little. Beat the cream cheese until light and fluffy, then add the cooled chocolate mixture and beat until soft and smooth. Set aside to cool completely, then spread evenly over the top of the cake.

Date roll

I received this recipe from my mother, Mrs Alma Winning (Theodore Branch, Qld).

LINDY CLEELAND, ORIELTON BRANCH, TAS.

½ cup sugar
1 cup dates
2 tablespoons butter
pinch of salt
1 teaspoon bicarbonate of soda
1 cup boiling water
1½ cups self-raising flour

SERVES 8

Preheat oven to 180°C. Grease a date roll tin with lid.

Combine sugar, dates, butter and salt. Sprinkle with bicarbonate of soda. Add the boiling water. Stir well, until butter is melted, then add sifted flour. Mix well.

Pour into prepared tin, but take out 1 tablespoon of mixture before sealing, so the tin does not pop its lid off. You can place this tablespoon of mixture on a tray in the oven beside the date roll tin, to give an indication of how well-cooked the actual cake will be.

For show purposes (when the date roll must have a level top and bottom) I reduce the amount of mixture and fill the tin only three-quarters full.

Golden syrup loaf

WILMA DELL, DEVONPORT BRANCH, TAS.

1 cup milk
1 tablespoon butter
2 tablespoons golden syrup
3 cups self-raising flour
1 cup sugar

MAKES 2 LOAVES (EACH SERVES 8–10)

Preheat oven to 180°C. Grease two loaf tins and line with aluminium foil.

Heat the milk with the butter and golden syrup in a saucepan until butter is melted. When milk is cool, add to the sifted flour and sugar. Mix well.

Pour into prepared loaf tins and bake for 45 minutes to 1 hour.

Black forest sponge cake

Black Forest cakes have become very popular in my family in recent years. This one has now replaced fruit cake for special occasions at our place. Although I know all about grams and my scales have both grams and ounces, when I make sponges I still use ounces.

MARION SPAULDING, HIGHCROFT/STORMLEA BRANCH, TAS.

- 5 eggs, separated
- 4 oz (110 g) sugar
- 4 oz (110 g) self-raising flour
- 2 tablespoons cocoa
- 3 tablespoons milk
- strawberries, extra cherries or shaved chocolate, to serve

filling

- 1 × 425-g can black cherries (preferably pitted)
- 6 teaspoons cornflour
- 4 teaspoons sugar
- 600 ml cream
- 1 tablespoon icing sugar (optional)
- 2 tablespoons cherry liqueur (optional)

SERVES 8

Preheat oven to 180°C. Grease a 20-cm round cake tin.

Using an electric beater, beat egg whites until they are stiff. Add the sugar in small quantities and make sure it is dissolved. Add egg yolks slowly and beat until thoroughly mixed. Clean off beaters, then add sifted flour and cocoa and milk to the egg mixture. Mix slowly and gently.

Pour into prepared tin and bake for 20–30 minutes, or until cooked. Turn out carefully and leave to cool. (Once cool, it can be frozen for later use.)

To make the filling, strain cherries and reserve juice, and remove pips if necessary. Keep 2 tablespoons juice in reserve, then mix remaining juice with the sifted cornflour and sugar in a saucepan and bring to the boil. Cook for about 2 minutes, stirring occasionally, until thickened. Add cherries and set aside to cool.

Beat cream until thick (adding icing sugar if desired). Split cake into three layers. Brush bottom layer with the reserved cherry juice (or cherry liqueur). Spread half the cherry filling evenly over the bottom layer, then spread 3 tablespoons of whipped cream over the top. Place second layer on and spread with remaining cherry mixture. Place top layer on and cover the whole cake with remaining cream (it can be piped or spread on). Decorate the top with strawberries, cherries or chocolate shavings.

Cinnamon scroll cake with coconut-ice frosting

PHYLLIS HINGSTON, SASSAFRAS/WESLEY VALE BRANCH, TAS.

1⅔ cups self-raising flour
¼ teaspoon salt
1 cup caster sugar
125 g butter or margarine
½ cup milk
2 eggs
few drops cochineal (pink food colouring)
1 dessertspoon ground cinnamon
1 dessertspoon coffee essence

coconut-ice frosting

2½ tablespoons milk
50 g copha
3 rounded tablespoons desiccated coconut
150 g icing sugar
vanilla essence, to taste
few drops of cochineal (pink food colouring)

SERVES 8–10

Preheat oven to 150°C. Grease an 18-cm square cake tin and line the base with baking paper.

Sift flour, salt and sugar into a bowl. Soften butter by beating slightly, then add to flour. Add three-quarters of the milk and beat for 1 minute using a wooden spoon or electric mixer on low speed. Add eggs and remaining milk and beat for 1 minute. Pour a quarter of the mixture into a separate basin and colour pink with the cochineal. Stir the cinnamon and coffee essence into the remaining mixture and place into the prepared tin. Pour the pink mixture on top and swirl with a knife.

Bake for 40–45 minutes, then turn out onto a wire rack to cool. Cover with coconut ice frosting once cold.

To make the frosting, place milk, copha and coconut in a saucepan and stir over low heat until copha is just melted (do not allow to boil). Add sifted icing sugar and mix well, then stir in vanilla essence and colouring. Beat until thick enough to spread.

Sultana loaf

JUNE WEAVER, GEORGE TOWN BRANCH, TAS.

250 g sultanas
125 g butter
2 eggs
1½ cups sugar
1 cup self-raising flour
almond essence, to taste
1 teaspoon mixed spice

SERVES 8–10

Preheat fan-forced oven to 160°C. Grease one large or two small loaf pans.

Place sultanas in a saucepan, cover with water and boil for 5 minutes. Drain and use a knife to cut in the butter. Beat eggs and sugar, then mix with the sultanas. Add sifted flour, almond essence and mixed spice.

Pour into prepared pans and bake for 1–1½ hours for the large pan, or 30–45 minutes for the small pans.

Gill's cream cupcakes

ELAINE YOUD, DEVONPORT BRANCH, TAS.

1 cup sugar
2 eggs
1 cup cream
1½ cups self-raising flour
pinch of salt
vanilla essence, to taste

MAKES 3 DOZEN

Preheat the oven to 190–200°C (fan-forced). Line three muffin pans with patty cases.

Beat the sugar and eggs well. Add cream, sifted flour, salt and vanilla.

Spoon mixture into patty cases and bake for 20 minutes.

Chocolate apple cake

This is Auntie Gwen Harris's recipe.

MRS ANNETTE FERGUSSON, ORIELTON BRANCH, TAS.

1 cup sugar
2 cups plain flour
1 teaspoon baking powder
1 teaspoon ground allspice
1 teaspoon ground nutmeg
1 teaspoon ground cinnamon
3 dessertspoons cocoa
125 g butter or margarine
1½ cups warm stewed apples, mixed with 1 teaspoon bicarbonate of soda
½ cup raisins
½ cup chopped walnuts
chocolate icing (page 176), with a little rum flavouring added
extra walnuts, for decorating

SERVES 8

Preheat oven to 160°C. Grease and line an 18-cm square cake tin.

Sift all dry ingredients together. Mix margarine with the stewed apples in a large bowl. Add dry ingredients to apple mixture and combine, then add raisins and walnuts and mix well.

Place mixture in prepared cake tin and bake in the oven for 45–60 minutes, or until a skewer inserted into the middle of the cake comes out clean.

When cake has cooled, ice with chocolate rum icing. Top with chopped walnuts.

Apricot loaf

GWYNETH WATKINS, GEORGE TOWN BRANCH, TAS.

1 egg

2 tablespoons softened butter

1 cup sugar

¾ cup dried apricots, diced and soaked in ¼ cup water

1 cup self-raising flour

½ teaspoon salt

½ cup milk

SERVES 8–10

Preheat oven to 160–180°C. Grease a loaf tin.

Cream the egg, butter and sugar. Add apricots and their liquid. Stir in sifted flour, salt and milk. Pour into prepared tin and bake for 1 hour.

Cherry cake

I usually use glacé cherries in this cake, but it is equally delicious with home-grown cherries. (Note that Kentish cherries will need a bit more sugar as they can be bitter.)

JANET AVERY, LATROBE BRANCH, TAS.

- 110 g softened butter
- 2 tablespoons sugar or sweetener
- 3 eggs, beaten
- 1½ cups self-raising flour
- ¼–½ cup milk
- ½ × 85-g packet cherry jelly crystals
- 2 tablespoons chopped almonds or walnuts
- 100 g cherries

SERVES 8

Preheat oven to 180°C. Grease a 20-cm cake tin.

Cream butter and sugar, then beat in eggs one at a time, beating well after each addition. Add sifted flour alternately with milk until well combined. Fold in jelly crystals, nuts and cherries.

Spoon into prepared tin and bake for about 45 minutes.

Caramel sponge

EILEEN McMULLEN, RANELAGH BRANCH, TAS.

1 tablespoon plain flour
¾ cup custard powder
½ teaspoon cream of tartar
1 teaspoon bicarbonate of soda
3 eggs
½ cup caster sugar
1 tablespoon hot golden syrup

SERVES 8

Preheat oven to 160°C. Grease or line a 20-cm sponge pan.

Sift together flour, custard powder, cream of tartar and bicarbonate of soda. Sift mixture twice more. In a separate bowl, beat eggs, add caster sugar and beat until creamy. Fold in flour mixture. Add hot golden syrup last and mix.

Pour mixture into prepared pan. Bake for approximately 20 minutes, or until cooked. Leave to cool in the tin for 5–10 minutes before turning out onto a wire rack.

Spiced pumpkin muffins

A favourite for all the family.

EDNA O'NEILL, CLOYNA BRANCH, QLD

125 g softened butter
¼ cup castor sugar
2 eggs
¼ cup golden syrup
1 cup pumpkin purée
½ cup chopped dates
½ cup mixed peel
2½ cups self-raising flour
½ teaspoon ground cinnamon
½ teaspoon ground nutmeg
½ teaspoon ground ginger
¼ teaspoon bicarbonate of soda
cinnamon sugar

MAKES 10–12

Preheat oven to 200°C. Grease a muffin pan.

Thoroughly blend the butter and sugar. Beat in eggs, golden syrup and pumpkin purée. Mix in the dates and mixed peel. Sift together the flour, spices and bicarbonate of soda, and fold into the mixture.

Spoon mixture into the prepared pan and sprinkle with cinnamon sugar. Bake for 20–25 minutes.

Banana fruit loaf

One day I thought I would add some overripe bananas to the fruit loaf recipe I usually make, instead of throwing them out. A tasty moist loaf resulted, so I continued to make this version. I have also discovered that eggs are not essential for a great result.

SUSAN HOLME, YUNGABURRA BRANCH, QLD

2 cups dates or mixed dried fruits of your choice
½ cup chopped glacé ginger
½ cup sugar
2 teaspoons bicarbonate of soda
110 g butter
2 cups boiling water
2 very ripe bananas, mashed
1 cup crushed pecan nuts
2 eggs, lightly beaten (optional)
2 cups self-raising flour
1 teaspoon ground cinnamon
1 teaspoon ground nutmeg

MAKES 2 LOAVES
(EACH SERVES 8–10)

Preheat oven to 170°C. Grease two loaf tins and line with non-stick baking paper.

Chop dried fruits and ginger and place in a bowl with the sugar, bicarbonate of soda and butter. Pour in boiling water and set aside to cool. Add bananas and pecan nuts to cooled fruit, then mix in eggs (if using) and lastly add the sifted flour and spices. Mix well.

Spoon into prepared tins, place on the middle shelf of the oven and bake for 30–40 minutes. Cool in the tins for 10 minutes before turning out.

Serve sliced and buttered for smoko or afternoon tea. (This loaf freezes well – wrap cooled cake in greaseproof paper and foil and place in a plastic bag in the freezer.)

Cinnamon cake

JOAN BEITZEL, FORREST BEACH BRANCH, NORTH QLD

110 g softened butter
1 cup caster sugar
1 teaspoon vanilla essence
3 eggs
1 cup self-raising flour
¾ cup plain flour
1 tablespoon ground cinnamon
¼ cup milk
mock cream (page 179)
chocolate icing (page 176)

SERVES 8–12

Preheat the oven to 180°C. Lightly grease a 28-cm × 18-cm lamington tin and line with greased paper.

Cream butter, add sugar and vanilla, beating until light and fluffy. Add eggs one at a time, beating well after each addition. Fold in sifted flours and cinnamon alternately with the milk.

Place mixture into prepared lamington tin and bake for 30–35 minutes. When cold, cut in half and join with mock cream, and ice with chocolate icing.

Hummingbird cake

NOELA MACLEOD, ESSENDON BRANCH, VIC.

540 g plain flour

400 g caster sugar

1 teaspoon bicarbonate of soda

1 teaspoon ground cinnamon

1 teaspoon ground ginger

3 eggs

1 cup canola oil

1 teaspoon vanilla essence

3 large ripe bananas, chopped

80 g pecan nuts, roughly chopped

250 g tinned crushed pineapple with juice

frosting

50 g softened butter

⅓ cup sour cream

375 g softened cream cheese

180 g icing sugar

lemon zest, to taste

1 tablespoon lemon juice

topping

1 large banana, sliced and tossed in lemon juice

1 star fruit, sliced

¼ pineapple, peeled and cut into decorative wedges

1 mango, peeled and sliced

pulp and juice of 2 passionfruits

SERVES 12–16

Preheat oven to 160°C. Grease and line the base of a 25-cm round cake tin.

To make the cake, sift the dry ingredients into a large bowl, stir in the eggs and oil and combine well. Mix in the vanilla essence, chopped bananas, pecans and pineapple and juice.

Pour batter into prepared cake tin and bake for 1¼ hours. Allow cake to cool in the tin for 15 minutes before turning out onto a wire rack.

To make the frosting, cream the butter, sour cream and cream cheese until fluffy. Add sifted icing sugar and mix gently to combine. Stir in lemon zest and juice. Refrigerate until ready to use. (Allow 10 minutes for frosting to soften to room temperature before spreading onto the cake.)

When cake is cool, cut in half horizontally. Spread the bottom half with a layer of cream-cheese frosting about 1 cm thick, then top with sliced banana. Place the other half of the cake on top and spread remaining frosting over cake surface. Decorate with the remaining fresh fruit and serve.

Orange date cake

This recipe has been passed down by my mother.

JUDY PRATT, DARWIN BRANCH, NT

110 g softened butter

110 g caster sugar

grated zest of 1 orange

2 eggs

170 g self-raising flour

pinch of salt

¼ cup milk

vanilla icing (page 180) or orange icing (page 179)

desiccated coconut (optional)

date filling

a little less than 100 g chopped dates

1 teaspoon grated orange zest

1 dessertspoon honey

a little less than ½ cup boiling water

SERVES 8–10

Preheat oven to 180°C. Grease a ring tin.

Cream butter, sugar and zest until fluffy. Add eggs one at a time, beating well after each addition. Fold in sifted flour and salt alternately with the milk.

To make the date filling, combine dates, orange zest and honey in a bowl and pour on the hot water. Leave to cool. When cold, beat to a pulp (it should have the consistency of jam.)

Place half the cake mixture in prepared tin, spread date mixture evenly over, then add remainder of cake mixture. Bake for 30–40 minutes.

When cool, you can ice with plain vanilla icing with a sprinkle of coconut, or orange icing.

(Note: I used to use plain flour with 2 teaspoons baking powder added, but these days I use self-raising flour.)

Pastry cake

JANET AVERY, LATROBE BRANCH, TAS.

1 cup sugar
50 g softened butter
1 egg
½ cup milk
1 cup self-raising flour

pastry

50 g butter, chopped
¾ cup self-raising flour
milk

filling

about ¼ cup raspberry or strawberry jam
about ½ cup sultanas

SERVES 8–10

Preheat oven to 180°C. Grease a 30-cm × 25-cm Swiss roll tin.

First make the pastry. Rub butter into sifted flour until crumbly, then add enough milk to make a firm dough. Roll out and use to line the Swiss roll tin.

Spread pastry with jam and sprinkle with sultanas.

To make the cake batter, cream the sugar and butter, then beat in egg. Add milk and sifted flour and fold gently until smooth. Spread mixture over the jam and sultana filling. Bake for 30–45 minutes, until browned on top.

Marble cake

ELAINE YOUD, DEVONPORT BRANCH, TAS.

- 170 g softened butter
- 230 g sugar
- 3 eggs
- 340 g self-raising flour
- small cup of milk
- 1 dessertspoon cocoa
- vanilla essence, to taste
- few drops cochineal (pink food colouring)
- chocolate icing (page 176)

SERVES 8–10

Preheat the oven to 180°C (fan-forced). Grease a 20-cm square cake tin.

Cream the butter and sugar well. Add eggs one by one, until well combined. Lastly add the sifted flour and milk. Divide mixture into three bowls – add sifted cocoa to one, vanilla to one and cochineal to the other.

Place the three mixtures alternately into the prepared tin. Bake for 1 to 1½ hours. Remove from oven, and when cold cover with chocolate icing.

Picnic cake

Kay Chalk from Mount Gambier gave me this recipe ten years ago. I find it is a great cake to take on holidays. It's very easy, and no icing is required.

WENDY WHITE, DARWIN BRANCH, NT

1½ cups boiling water
70 g dates, chopped
1¾ teaspoons bicarbonate of soda
¾ cup softened butter
1 cup sugar
2 eggs
2 cups plain flour
½ teaspoon salt
½ cup chocolate chips
½ cup sugar
½ cup broken walnuts

SERVES 8–12

Preheat oven to 175°C. Lightly grease a 28-cm × 18-cm lamington tin.

Pour boiling water over dates and stir in 1 teaspoon of the bicarbonate of soda. Allow to stand until cool.

Cream the butter and sugar. Beat in eggs, then remaining bicarbonate of soda, sifted four and salt. Fold in date mixture.

Pour into prepared tin and sprinkle over the chocolate chips, sugar and walnuts. Bake for 35–45 minutes. Serve hot with whipped cream as a dessert, or cold as a cake.

Easy sultana cake

JOYCE GOOS, VALENTINE PLAINS BRANCH, QLD

1 x 375-g packet sultanas
230 g butter
230 g sugar
1 teaspoon lemon essence
1 teaspoon vanilla essence
5 eggs
285 g plain flour
40 g self-raising flour

SERVES 8

Preheat the oven to 175°C. Grease a 20-cm cake tin.

Soak the sultanas in warm water for 2–3 hours. Cream butter and sugar, then beat in lemon and vanilla essences. Add the 5 eggs and beat well. Stir in drained sultanas, then sift in flours and mix to combine.

Pour into prepared cake tin. Bake in the preheated oven for 15 minutes, then reduce oven temperature to 160°C and cook for another 1¼ hours.

Quick orange cake

This cake is a favourite of my sister-in-law, and has been passed down by her mother.

JUDY PRATT, DARWIN BRANCH, NT

170 g margarine
170 g sugar
2 eggs
juice of 1 orange
½ cup milk
1½ cups self-raising flour

SERVES 8

Preheat the oven to 180°C. Grease a 20-cm cake tin.

Beat margarine and sugar to a cream. Add eggs one at a time, beating well. Hand beat in the orange juice until soft and fluffy. Add milk and sifted flour alternately, and beat until combined.

Place in prepared tin and bake for 25 minutes.

Passionfruit cake

JOYCE POLGLASE, GEORGE TOWN BRANCH, TAS.

125 g softened butter
¾ cup caster sugar
2 eggs
2 cups self-raising flour
½ cup milk
pulp of 3 passionfruit
whipped cream (optional)
passionfruit icing (page 180)

SERVES 8

Preheat oven to 180°C. Grease a 20-cm cake tin.

Cream butter and sugar until light and fluffy. Add eggs one at a time, beating well after each addition. Stir in sifted flour alternately with milk. Stir in passionfruit pulp.

Place mixture into prepared tin. Bake for 50 minutes.

Once cold, cake can be split and filled with whipped cream. Ice with passionfruit icing.

German cake

NOELA MACLEOD, ESSENDON BRANCH, VIC.

45 g butter
½ cup warm mashed potato
¾ cup sugar
1 egg, beaten
½ cup sultanas
2 cups self-raising flour
1 teaspoon ground nutmeg
1 teaspoon mixed spice
1 teaspoon ground cinnamon
1 cup milk

topping

90 butter, chopped
1 cup plain flour
½ cup sugar
¾ teaspoon ground cinnamon

SERVES 12–14

Preheat oven to 180°C. Grease a slab tin or lamington tin.

Mix butter into warm mashed potato, then add sugar and egg. Mix in the sultanas, sifted flour and spices, and then milk. Spoon mixture into prepared tin.

To make topping, rub butter into sifted dry ingredients until crumbly. Sprinkle topping over cake mixture. Bake for 45 minutes.

Delicious date and ginger cake

BEVERLEY LEE, CENTRAL COAST BRANCH, TAS.

1 cup chopped dates
1 cup soft brown sugar
½ cup crystallised ginger
110 g butter, chopped
1 teaspoon bicarbonate of soda
1½ cups self-raising flour
1 egg, beaten

SERVES 8

Preheat oven to 180°C (fan-forced 160°C). Grease an 18-cm square cake tin.

Put dates, sugar, ginger, butter and 1 cup water in a saucepan. Bring to the boil, then take off the stove and add the bicarbonate of soda. Stir, then add sifted flour and egg and mix well.

Pour mixture into the prepared tin and bake for about 45 minutes.

American quick bread

This is the recipe I use when making loaves for cake stalls or catering – it is so quick and easy. I usually double the mixture and make two at a time.

ELAINE YOUD, DEVONPORT BRANCH, TAS.

55 g butter
1 cup dates or mixed dried fruit
1 cup cold water
¾ cup sugar
1 tablespoon mixed spice
2 cups self-raising flour

SERVES 8–10

Preheat oven to 180°C. Grease a loaf tin.

Place all ingredients (except flour) in a saucepan and bring to the boil. Take off the heat, then add sifted flour and mix well.

Pour mixture into prepared tin and bake for 30 minutes.

Chocolate icing

2 cups icing sugar
4 tablespoons cocoa
2 teaspoons melted butter
3–4 tablespoons warm water

Sift icing sugar and cocoa into a bowl. Add melted butter to warm water, then stir enough into the sugar mix to make a smooth paste.

Chocolate butter icing

60 g dark cooking chocolate, chopped
125 g softened butter
2 cups icing sugar
1–2 tablespoons warm milk

Melt chocolate in a double boiler over simmering water or on MEDIUM in the microwave. Set aside to cool.

Cream the butter, then gradually add sifted icing sugar alternately with milk, until soft and creamy. Beat in cooled melted chocolate until smooth.

Cream-cheese frosting

NOELA MACLEOD, ESSENDON BRANCH, VIC.

90 g softened cream cheese
1 cup icing sugar
½ teaspoon vanilla essence
1 teaspoon honey
milk

Beat the cream cheese until light, then beat in sifted icing sugar, vanilla essence and honey, adding a little milk to give a spreading consistency.

Custard

2 eggs
1 tablespoon caster sugar
1 cup milk
few drops vanilla extract

Whisk the eggs and sugar gently in a mixing bowl. Heat the milk and vanilla until warm, then remove from heat and add to egg mixture. Tip mixture back into the saucepan and, stirring constantly, bring to the boil. Turn down heat immediately and simmer, stirring continuously, until custard is thick enough to coat the back of a spoon. Serve warm or cold.

If serving the custard cold, whisk the still-warm custard in a stainless steel bowl set over a bowl of ice, until cool (this stops the custard splitting).

Lemon or orange icing

- 1 teaspoon softened butter
- 2 cups icing sugar
- 2 tablespoons freshly squeezed lemon or orange juice

Beat together butter and sifted icing sugar, gradually adding the juice to achieve a spreading consistency.

Mock cream

If you prefer, you can use fresh whipped cream instead of mock cream.

JOAN BEITZEL, FORREST BEACH BRANCH, NORTH QLD

- 2 tablespoons butter or margarine
- 2 tablespoons sugar
- 2 tablespoons hot water
- 2 tablespoons milk
- vanilla essence or food colouring (optional)

Cream butter and sugar well. Continue beating while you slowly add hot water alternately with milk, until all sugar is dissolved. Add vanilla essence and colouring as required.

Passionfruit icing

1 tablespoon softened butter
¼ cup passionfruit pulp
2 cups icing sugar

Combine butter and passionfruit. Gradually add the sifted icing sugar, stirring until you achieve a spreadable consistency.

Vanilla icing

2 teaspoons softened butter
2 cups icing sugar
½ teaspoon vanilla essence
2–3 tablespoons water or milk

Beat together butter and sifted icing sugar, add vanilla, then gradually add enough water or milk to achieve a spreading consistency.

Conversions

(All conversions are approximate)

Measures for cake tins

cm (centimetres)	in (inches)
5	2
8	3
10	4
13	5
15	6
18	7
20	8
23	9
25	10
28	11
30	12

Oven temperatures

°C (Celsius)	°F (Fahrenheit)
100	210
135	275
150	300
160	320
170	340
175	350
180	355
190	375
200	390
205	400
230	445

Liquid measures

ml (millilitres)	fl oz (fluid ounces – UK)
50	1¾
200	7
300	10½
360	12⅔
400	14
600	1 pt 1 fl oz
1000 (1 litre)	1 pt 15 fl oz

Weights

g (grams)	oz (ounces)
30	1
55–60	2
90	3
100	3½
110	4
125	4½
150	5
230	8
250	9
340	12
400	14
450	16 (1 lb)
500	1 lb 1½ oz

Tip: *To test that a cake is cooked, insert a thin skewer into the centre of the cake; if it comes out clean, the cake is ready.*

Index

PENGUIN BOOKS

Published by the Penguin Group
Penguin Group (Australia)
250 Camberwell Road, Camberwell, Victoria 3124, Australia
(a division of Pearson Australia Group Pty Ltd)

New York Toronto London Dublin New Delhi Auckland Johannesburg

Penguin Books Ltd, Registered Offices: 80 Strand, London, WC2R 0RL, England

First published by Penguin Group (Australia) in association with the Country Women's Association of Australia, 2009

10 9 8 7 6 5 4 3

Many of the recipes included in this book have been passed on to the contributors from family and friends, or adapted from recipes collected over the years from magazines and other publications.

Many thanks to CSR for generously providing sugar for the photoshoot.

Text and cover design by Claire Tice & Marley Flory © Penguin Group (Australia), 2009
Photography by Julie Renouf
Food styling by Lee Blaylock
Typeset in Avenir by Post Pre-press Group, Brisbane, Queensland
Scanning and separations by Splitting Image P/L, Clayton, Victoria
Printed and bound by South China Printing Co Ltd, China

National Library of Australia
Cataloguing-in-Publication data:

CWA Cakes
ISBN 978 0 14 320230 1
Includes index
Cake
Country Women's Association of Australia

641.8653

penguin.com.au